Witness to Resilience:

Stories of Intimate Violence

For The Trinity Staff
With Respect —

Jane Seskin

JANE SESKIN

Praise for WITNESS TO RESILIENCE

"Jane Seskin's masterful poems tell of relationships filled with the cruelty and shame that violence bestows on its victims ... yet the hope of a path toward non-violence is ever-present. Seskin retells these complex journeys in crystal clear, hard-hitting yet beautiful poetry."

> Mary Haviland, Esq.
> Executive Director, New York City Alliance
> Against Sexual Assault

"An intimate look at the world in which survivors live, struggle, tell their stories and ultimately prevail. These poems transform the survivor's experiences into words that pack a visceral punch laced with hope."

> Patricia Carey, MD
> Medical Director, Roosevelt Hospital
> Emergency Department, New York City

Printed in the United States of America

ISBN-13: 978-1483940205

Books By Jane Seskin

Novelizations

Fantasy Island I

Fantasy Island II

Breaking Up

Poetry

A Time To Love

Living Single

Getting My Head Straight

Nonfiction

Young Widow

Older Women/Younger Men

More Than Mere Survival: Conversations With Women
    Over 65

Alone Not Lonely: Independent Living for Women Over 50

The Comfort Book

CONTENTS

Foreword

Witness To Resilience is about everyday women who have endured their abuse in silence and secrecy. They're your mother, sister, daughter, aunt, friend, neighbor, and colleague.

After more than two decades as a therapist, I *know* personal change is possible. I continue to be hopeful as I see women leave counseling transformed, both physically and emotionally. These women have reclaimed their bodies and their souls. In the process they've developed a stronger sense of self. They've learned a hard-won truth: abuse in any form is disrespectful, debilitating, dangerous, and has nothing to do with love.

Witness To Resilience is a blueprint to where the minefields are. It's a companion that whispers in your ear:

1) You are not alone. Other women have felt the fear, the humiliation, and the pain.

2) You are not crazy. What is happening to you is truly happening.

3) You are not to blame. The abuse is not your fault.

4) You are deserving of respect. You can/will survive this.

We professionals, family members, friends, neighbors, and co-workers can tell women that when they give voice to the violence they will be heard, believed and helped. And in raising their voices, their isolation will begin to be over. By speaking the unspeakable, we can end the violence that has diminished so many lives.

Jane Seskin

(Please note that the survivors I talk about in *Witness To Resilience* are women. This does not preclude the fact that abuse survivors are also men.)

DOMESTIC VIOLENCE

is an intentional pattern of coercive behaviors (i.e., verbal, emotional, psychological, physical, sexual, economic) to maintain power and control over one's intimate partner. Partners can be married, living together, separated or dating, heterosexual, gay or lesbian.

RESILIENCE

is the ability to become strong, healthy or successful again after something bad or traumatic happens.

Home

I never thought
of the kitchen as a battlefield
with hot foods,
dishes, pots and silverware
used as weapons.

I never imagined
a broken mirror could scar flesh,
a bedroom pillow could smother a breath,
a curtain rod could gouge out an eye.

I never realized
the handy tool chest
could be
so lethal;

roach spray could blind,
hammers could break fingers
and screwdrivers could puncture
arms, legs, breasts.

I never thought,
imagined,
or realized,

but now I do,
since I started listening
to women

talk
about
the violence.

Talking Violence

I tell the police, the doctors
and anyone who will listen
the stories of women
who cannot speak …

whose lips are swollen shut,
teeth knocked out by a punch,
or ground down
from clenching and grimacing,

throat sore from swallowing,
inhaling years of insults
and indignities
yet not answering back,

nor telling,
because then
there would be more
violence

or, as Sonia whispered
in my quiet office
one early summer day,
her very deep, real fear:

"I'll be murdered."

Beginnings

It may be as simple
as a 'look'
or withholding conversation,
affection, presence,

or subtle power
and control
over friendships,
money, choices made.

You feel something is off.
You begin to be watchful,
hesitant, careful
in your behavior.

Not a punch
has been thrown
nor a face slapped,
yet the dance has begun.

This is not the time
for you
to shut down,
ignore, deny.

This is the time
to be conscious,
to question
and get help,

before
the Krazy
glue
dries.

Bread Crumbs

Her life story
of spousal abuse

poured
from swollen lips
onto the floor
of my therapy office

littering the rug
til the end of the day

when I bent down to examine
the exclamation points
of violence
she'd left behind

and the question marks
surrounding
the meaning
of love.

Sitting With The Flowers

Cut with knife,
bottle, high-heel shoe,
the battered women talk
of violence
    surrounded by tulips.

Burned with cigarettes,
beaten with hammers,
scalded with hot oil,
spat on,
they reveal their fear,
anger, sadness and secrets
    surrounded by roses
    and hydrangeas.

The weeks go by,
the office flowers
change
    and there are daffodils,
    poppies, lilies, carnations.

Flowers to calm the soul,
flowers so strong
they
    will
        not
            wilt

in spite of –

    all the horrors
    they hear
    in this room.

A Rationale - #1

In session today

I asked Tina
about the gauze bandage
wrapped around the palm
of her right hand.

She looked down
at it resting in her lap,
turned it over, winced in pain,
then explained the injury.
.
"Over the weekend
when I was smoking,
Teddy slapped
the cigarette out of my mouth

and forced me
to put it out
on the floor,
with the palm of my hand.

He told me
smoking
wasn't good
for me.

He did it for my health."

And This Is What He Said

Last client of the day
recounts a week
of verbal and emotional abuse

where her husband's words,
yes his words,
lacerated her heart.

He said to her:
    You stink. You're fat.
    You're evil.

He said to her:
    You're a bad mother. A whore.
    An effing bitch.

He said to her:
    Clean the house. Clean the kids.
    Clean yourself. It's all a mess.

He said to her
    you better remember this:
        you'll never find anyone
        as good as me,

        and no one else
        will want you.

We talk.
She leaves the session
and all I want to do

is go cry in a shower.

The Rules

It's not allowed
because he says so.

Don't paint
your lips and cheeks.
Don't wear clothes
that show your body.

It's not allowed
because he says so.

Don't watch television
without permission.
Don't make phone calls
when he's at work.

It's not allowed
because he says so.

Don't talk
to the neighbors.
Don't leave
the block.

It's not allowed
because he says so
because he says
he says so
he says

No!

Dismissed

Elaine told me

her husband
made her
eat dinner

sitting
in
the
bathtub

because
he said

she was

a
pig.

Seduction

First session
of the week.

I get it Dear Lucy
that your love-hunger
is filled

with his constant,
persistent,
unwavering attention.

77 texts,
43 voice mails
in   one   day!

Oh yes the flattery,
the pursuit,
the possibility.

The emptiness
is nourished.

How very exciting, but …
I've heard it
before.

I've seen it.
I'm telling you
Sweetheart,

do not swallow!

Law Enforcement

In the beginning
she said
she felt proud.

She's married to a policeman,
a "peace officer"

who held her head down
in the toilet and flushed.

She's married to a policeman
sworn to "protect and serve"

who tied her hands and feet
to the bedposts

and shoved a nightstick
up her vagina.

She's married to a policeman
who made her lick
the barrel of his gun

on the night
he was awarded
a commendation

for
'Heroism'.

The Child Comes To A Session

Nine years old.
Quiet.
Well-behaved.
Straight A's.

Sits hunched over
the side of my desk,
magic markers in hand.
Draws houses.

Draws multi-level houses.
Draws houses deep in the forest
surrounded by tall gates.
Wants to be an architect.

I ask her why.
"Because," she answers,
head down, still drawing.
"Because why?" I continue.

"So I can build a house
some place far away,
for my Mom
and me,

a house
where my Father
will never
find us."

My Anxiety

Early on
on weekends,
on the weekends,
every ambulance
I saw,

every siren
I heard
was ... a reminder,
cause to worry

to worry
and wonder
if someone I had seen
was in trouble ...

beaten,

bloody,

broken.

Evolution

Left for dead,
found by son,
9-1-1 to hospital.

Eye removed,
knife wounds closed,
hundreds of stitches
pulling in pain.

Husband jailed,
safe at last,
agrees to talk
about her life.

Body heals,
emotions managed,
prosthetic eye
proves a plus.

Stands in court,
before the jury,
removes eye
for show and tell.

Verdict decided,
Judge declares,
twelve to twenty
years for him.

She …
gets
the rest
of her life.

Flashbacks

Bruises fade,
broken bones heal,
but memories
of abuse ...

memories of abuse ...

attach like flypaper
 to the brain,
 searing the soul,
 scarring the heart.

Memories of abuse ...
 infiltrate the present
 maybe not daily
 but frequently enough

and dictate the future
 can I
 should I
 trust this person?

Memories of abuse ...
 hidden away
 undercover
 everlasting.

Testimony

Tell,
please tell.
Tell.
You must tell
someone.

Tell the secret
to a friend,
relative,
co-worker,
someone,
anyone,
just ... tell.

Talk.
Talk the pain
heal the heart.

Talk.
Talk the hurt
heal the head.

Tell now.

Get up.
Do it.

Tell.

Now.

Yes!

Confirmation

Evil
is in my therapy office
right now

leeching off the woman
who has come to tell me
of her abuser.

I can smell the fear on her
attaching to the walls
like a veil of cobwebs

and see
the blood
snaking along the carpet

as I imagine
years of broken limbs
and battered body parts

and I blink back
as she
tears up –

this parallel process
where I mirror
with my face

the horror

of her life
stories.

Relatively Speaking

His family says:
  Drop the charges,
  the bruises will heal.
  He didn't break
  anything on you.

His family promises:
  He won't hurt you
  again ...
  when he refuses
  to make that claim.

His family offers:
  A new TV,
  cell phone
  and a winter coat
  to sweeten the deal.

His family pleads:
  Forgive ...
  Forgive ...
  Forgive ...
  and forget.

But she can't
  not this time,
  number seven
  times hurt,

and she won't
drop the charges,

Not
This
Time.

Discipline

I witness
the grown woman,

daughter of a batterer
recounts kneeling
on a pile of rice
on the kitchen floor
with a pot on her head.

"Stay there," he yelled
at the seven-year old.
"Back straight.
Stay there.
Don't cry!"

And she stayed,
knees bleeding
til she fell over.

Now red-faced,
all these years later
sobbing, possessed,
crying out in my office
for the first time:

"Daddy,
No More!"

It Is What It Is

Stop working
so hard
to discuss, explain,
convince, cajole,
argue, apologize,
bargain, bluff,
fix, change,
help
him out.

Stop looking
for the key
to unlock
his conscience.

In your head,
in your heart,
you know
who he is.

So back away
Dear One,

and
save
yourself.

Ceremony

It is our final therapy session,
week number 12.

We walk, she and I,
to the bathroom.

I carry a picture of Tom,
her abusive ex.

I cut him
into pieces of limbs

that fall down
to the plate in the sink

and invite her
to cut off his head.

I hand her
a book of matches

so she can turn his image
to ashes,

and as we watch him
shrivel and disappear

she haltingly,
tearfully,

says
her good-bye.

Intimidation

One evening,

the doctor/surgeon/husband
cut the heads
off three of his wife's stuffed animals,
(the teddy bears)

and left their small bodies
resting

against the silk-clad pillows
on their bed.

Possession

Each morning

before she leaves
for work,

she must bend
from the waist
in front
of him.

If he sees
cleavage,

she will
have to
run upstairs
to change.

"No one,"
he tells her,
"gets to see
what's mine."

Lightning

She needed
to sleep.

She had a job interview
first thing in the morning.

It meant more money,
more responsibility.

She needed
her sleep.

He sat on a bedroom chair
by the light switch,

flicking it on and off
every few minutes

throughout the night,
this most important night,

when she really,
really needed
to sleep.

Intention

The issue is not
why
he's abusive.

The issue is
when you tell him
to stop, to change
his behavior,

he *chooses*

not to.

This Is So Not About You

It doesn't matter
what you did,
or said.

It doesn't matter
who you talked to,
or who spoke to you.

It doesn't matter
if you gained
or lost weight,
if you're a good cook
or not,
whether your home
is spotless or messy.

YOU
are not the reason
He hits you.

HE
is the reason
HE hits you.

Time-Out

During this work week
I talked down a batterer
holding a gun
to his wife's head,

counseled a battered man
to leave his abusive wife
and fight for custody
of his children,

found clothing for a woman
who walked into a shelter
black-and-blue brave
carrying her baby,

and sat at a hospital bedside,
holding the hand of a woman
pushed out a window
by her ex-husband.

Sometimes, sometimes the life stories
are so disturbing in their brutality,
so emotionally decimating
that I long to flee, to run away,

to take a running jump
out the window of my office …
only the office
is on the first floor

so instead … in these moments

I close the door,
put my feet up on the couch,
sip from a mug of cold coffee,
turn on the radio

and wrap my soul in music.

List/Serve

Make a list
Sweet Laura.

Make a list
of every single verbal,
emotional,
and physical bruise.

List the words,
the behaviors,
the assaults
to body and soul.

Carry the list
in your pocket.
Look
at it.

As you read
and reflect,
notice each and every
body memory.

Let the list
call
you
to action.

Let the list
set you free.

The Group For Battered Women

They sit together
week after week
in my office,

tall and short, fat and thin,
young and old,
different, yet the same
with violence the great leveler

and they talk, cry and rage
in this room
where they are safe
about peculiarities, similarities,
mutualities

and surprise surprise
laugh,
laugh hard and joyously,
laugh with tears
racing down their cheeks

at life
in the moment,
understood
right here, right now
by their sister-circle

because otherwise …

otherwise …
otherwise
they'd go crazy.

A Rationale - #2

I asked the members
of a battered women's group
to bring in their wedding pictures.

I wanted them to be able
to acknowledge a time
of hope and joy,

that we all understood
and recognized
the abuse wasn't 24/7.

When Denise passed around her picture
you could see the shadow of a bruise
under her right eye.

She told us
Bill had gotten angry
and punched her.

Betsy wanted to know
why
she'd gone through with the wedding.

"I couldn't back out," Denise answered.
"My parents
paid a fortune

for the celebration."

Suzanne

In my group
one winter evening

Suzanne says to me:
"You look pale.
You look like shit."

The group
is silent.
Stunned.

I breathe.
Take   my   time.

"And, if I look like shit?" I ask,
"what does that mean
to you?"

"I don't know," she answers.

"Well perhaps you think
I won't be able
to take care of you?"

She pauses,
then nods.

The group releases
a collective sigh
and we continue.

And I, well I vow
to wear more makeup.

Group Intervention

They want
to poison
cut
beat
burn
shoot
their abusers

and I encourage
them
to talk,
plan,
figure out
the perfect act
of revenge.

At the end
of the evening
I say
to my group
of battered women:

"Everyone,
please remember
this is fantasy-
not action.

Ladies!
Are we clear?"

Action Plan

Get your life
back from him
any way
you can.

Take it
when he's not looking.

Grab it
when no one's around.

Smuggle it out
in pieces
if you have to.

Hug your one great life
hard and tight.
Own it straight up
from your toes
to the top of your head.

That's right.
Now
breathe deeply
and vow

to never, ever again
let disrespect
play with your spirit,
or tickle your skin.

Fearful

I'm afraid.

She tells me her husband
the batterer
has threatened to hurt me
for helping her.

I'm afraid

and look over my shoulder
when I leave my office
at the end of the day.

I'm afraid

he will cut me
the way he has
her.

I'm angry

he's made me

so afraid.

Present

I know I've become
more assertive
in my personal life.

"Please, don't point
your finger at me,"
I tell a friend, explaining
"it's a gesture of intimidation."

Then, as sole member
of the verbal police,

I'm acutely sensitive
to dismissive phrases
and conversation.

Words spoken
to disrespect,
I now label as such.

Bottom line?
I will not tolerate
bad behavior

from any one,
at any time,
in any place.

Hide-And-Seek

End
of first session.

She takes off
her right shoe
and puts my business card
under the inner sole.

She taps the shoe
so the insert
will lie flat
then puts it back on.

"It will
be safe,"
she tells me
with a smile.

"He never searches
my shoes."

TimeKeeper

The only flowers
she ever received

came after a beating.

Each bouquet she trimmed,
hung upside down to dry
stapled to the crown molding
in their bedroom.

Dinner guests
leaving their coats on the bed
would marvel
at the floral decoration.

When the room
was totally encircled
by the flowers,
she left her life.

Months later in therapy
she talked
about patience:
"I was getting myself ready

to walk out. I knew
looking at the flowers,
the time had come.

Enough
was finally enough."

And Then I Said ...

Carole came to see me
after she left a marriage
punctuated
by verbal and emotional abuse.

Elegant, understated,
she said: "I thought I was going crazy.
He'd be charming in public,
nasty, demeaning, withholding in private.

It was like I was living, existing,
with two different men.
Once, he didn't talk to me at home
for a period of two months."

During her time in therapy
she met a man.
Widower, kind, funny, good.
And they decided to marry.

On the small reception line,
standing on tiptoe to kiss his cheek,
I whispered
into the new husband's ear:

"If you hurt her
I will find out ...

and I will find you ..."

My Left Knee

Tripped and bruised my knee
a few days before my annual physical
with a doctor I liked
and respected.

The knee
was muddy yellow
and he never asked
what happened.

I felt anxious,
worried
on my way home,
then angry.

Called him up.
Said: "You never asked
about my knee.
I could have been
pushed down, assaulted."

He replied:
"Not you, Jane.
It wouldn't happen
to you."

"But Doc, then I am
just the one
you need to ask.
The one you don't expect."

Stop!

**No
to couples therapy
when violence is present.**

Your friend/partner/husband
needs to own
and be responsible
for his abusive behavior.

How can I
say it simply
and clearly enough?

He needs
to get counseling,
therapy,

and Sweetheart,
you too need
to work with someone,
to better inhabit your life.

Each of you
must learn
to know
and honor the self,

before you
work together
reframing
the relationship.

I
remain
hopeful.

The Practice Of Heart Health

stand still and breathe

sing, dance, laugh

collect friends

exercise curiosity

give away kindness

sit with your feelings

dream big

ask for help

be gentle with yourself

thank everyone

eat mindfully

stay open to possibility

have hope

climb your mountain,
whatever it may be ...

and always,
find safety and comfort
at home

The Take-Away

Repeat
3 times a day.

I'm grateful
to be alive.

I deserve to be treated
with kindness and respect.

The only person
I can change

is myself.

I know abuse.
I choose other,

different,
better.

Acknowledgments

A huge Thank You goes to the incredible, resilient
survivors I met and worked with in individual and group
sessions. They showed up. Week after week. To talk, to
plan, to act. They entrusted me with their life stories and
allowed me to offer them hope. I celebrate their courage.

I've been extremely fortunate to have had an ongoing,
creative, 20-year passionate conversation about violence
with colleagues, who became friends, at the Crime Victims
Treatment Center. We consulted with each other in
hallways, during lunch, between therapy sessions and after
hours. We were constantly looking for the best ways to
provide treatment. The clinical team was led by Susan
Xenarios, a Director whose inclusiveness and intellectual
foresight helped shape our work. Early teammates were
Andrea Dixon, Dr. Ruth Forero, and Louise Kindley. Lois
Orlin provided supervision. Over the years, Sally Clayton,
Dr. David Gandler, Bibi Geller, Erika Guzman, Lisa
Haileselassie, Amie Karp, Nilda Lopez, Kathy Rebillot,
Kerry Stout and Michael White joined in this collaborative
approach to healing. Off-site, I co-led a batterers group
with Jack Smith.

Melissa Mertz, Christine Nolin and Mary Triest are the
generous, spirited, meditative friends who've been there
from the beginning. I am grateful for their continuing
presence.

Other Dear Friends over the years listened, consoled, supported and brought laughter to my life. They include: Mary Anderson, Linda Breslau, Nancy Garrity, Mary Alice Kellogg, Barbara Niles, Pamela Nolan, Vera Ryersbach, Susan Schatz, Jane Sinnenberg, Naomi Taicher, Nicki Turano and Rose Weinstock.

The women of the Second Sunday of The Month Group helped me to detach and to listen to the music of a new life: Susan Borg, Roberta Brodfeld, Rima Greenberg, Toni Hall, Evelyn Eller Rosenbaum and Jane Waisman.

Acknowledgment to the University of Virginia Medical School Journal *Hospital Drive* (Issue #7) which first published the poem "Intimidation," and to the Vermont Studio Center for a poetry residency. Special thanks to poet/mentor Arthur Sze.

Thank you to Peter Hoffman for his editorial guidance and to Dear Friend Larry Sloan, reader extraordinaire and to Louise Kindley who patiently gave invaluable help and advice in preparing this manuscript. Cover design was created by the artist Francisco A. de León who has always respected the poetry.

Books To Inform, Inspire, Nourish

Al-Anon Family Group: *Courage To Change*

Anderson, Joan: *A Weekend To Change Your Life*

Bancroft, Lundy: *Why Does He Do That?*

Beattie, Melody: *Codependent No More*

Beck, Aaron: *Love Is Never Enough*

Breathnach, Sarah Ban: *Simple Abundance*

Cameron, Julia: *The Artist's Way*

Chodron, Pema: *The Places That Scare You*

Ely, Karen: *Breathing Space*

Engel, Beverly: *The Emotionally Abusive Relationship*

Evans, Patricia: *The Verbally Abusive Relationship*

Frankel, Viktor E.: *Man's Search For Meaning*

Goldberg, Natalie: *Writing Down The Bones*

Hanh, Thich Nhat: *Making Space*

Hendricks, Gay: *A Year Of Living Consciously*

Herman, Judith Lewis: *Trauma And Recovery*

Housden, Roger: *Ten Poems To Change Your Life*

Jones, Ann and Schechter, Susan: *When Love Goes Wrong*

Keillor, Garrison: *Good Poems*

Kornfield, Jack: *Buddha's Little Instruction Book*

Lamott, Anne: *Bird By Bird*

Lerner, Harriet: *The Dance Of Anger*

Lesser, Elizabeth: *Broken Open*

Lindbergh, Anne Morrow: *Gift From The Sea*

McGraw, Phillip: *Relationship Rescue*

Moore, Thomas: *Care Of The Soul*

O'Donohue, John: *To Bless The Space Between Us*

Oliver, Mary: *A Thousand Mornings*

Oriah Mountain Dreamer: *The Invitation*

Rilke, Maria Rainer: *Letters To A Young Poet*

Rubin, Gretchen: *The Happiness Project*

Seskin, Jane: *The Comfort Book*

Strayed, Cheryl: *Tiny Beautiful Things*

Walker, Lenore E.A.: *The Battered Woman Syndrome*

Weissman, Elaine: *Family And Friends' Guide to Domestic Violence*

Weitzman, Susan: *"Not To People Like Us"*

Wilson, Beth with Mo Therese Hannah: *He's Just No Good For You*

FOR INFORMATION AND HELP

National Domestic Violence Hotline: 1-800-799-7233

Rape, Abuse and Incest National Network
(www.RAINN.org)

National Sexual Assault Hotline: 1-800-656-4673

Elder Abuse Hotline: 1-888-800-1409

ABOUT THE AUTHOR

Jane Seskin is a licensed clinical social worker and the author of eleven books and numerous non-fiction articles. Her poetry has been published in magazines and journals and she was selected for a poetry residency to the Vermont Studio Center.

For 20 years she worked with survivors of violent crimes at the Crime Victims Treatment Center in New York City. She currently maintains a private psychotherapy and consultation practice with adult clients presenting a variety of issues including relationships, addiction and recovery, career strategies, divorce, aging, loss and bereavement.

In addition, she is the owner of plainjane-cards.com.

NOTES

NOTES

NOTES

NOTES

Made in the USA
Charleston, SC
27 June 2013

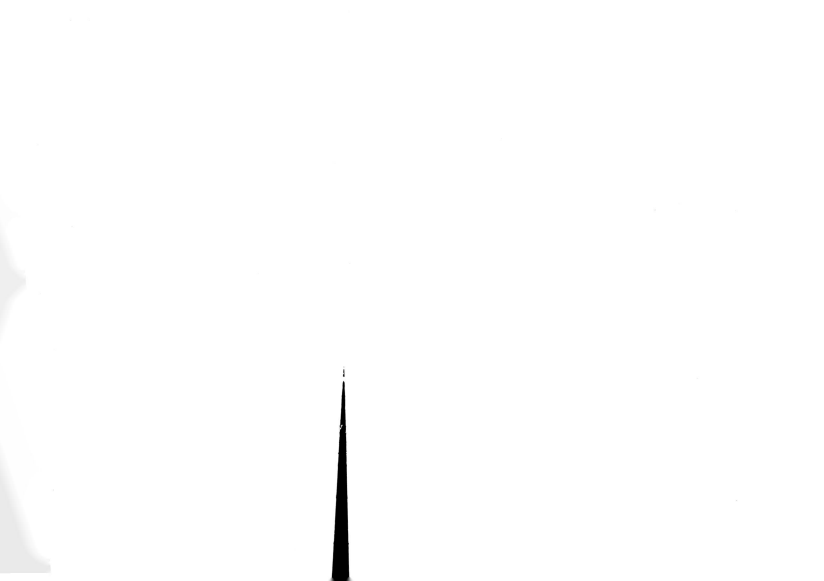

JANE
140 WEST END AVENUE,
NEW YORK, NEW YORK 10023-6144

TELEPHONE (212) 580-7841

October 1, 2013

Dear John,

October is Domestic Violence
Awareness Month.

I hope my new book will be
of interest to you and your
staff.

Sincerely,
Jane